COME
ON
SUCCESS
...FOR ALL

ASHU SHARMA

First published in India in 2019

ISBN: 978-81-94279990

Registered Address: 201A, SAS Tower, Sector 38, Gurgaon-122003

Printed at Thomson Press (India) LTD

I would like to dedicate this book to my loving husband 'Raj' and adorable daughter 'Anamika'

ACKNOWLEDGEMENT

I am very much grateful and hope that the readers will find the book really helpful in their journey towards success. I am thankful to everyone especially my family and friends. A special thanks to my brother, Dr. Bipan Sumbria (General Physician), who never fails to encourage me. I would have not been able to complete it without their support. I, humbly, dedicate my book to my husband, who has been the driving force in all my endeavours. It is his faith in me which made me believe in myself.

Thanks and regards

Ashu sharma

"Blind turns of my life, which I thought, were making me scared earlier, only after passing them I realised that they were beautifying my life in a different way."

CONTENT

Chapter I

Struggle Leads to Success

What impelled me to write this book? It was my own experience, while teaching students of different schools and colleges, I got to know that everyone has different calibre, intelligence, potential and the most significant was the opinion of their teachers/friends/parents about them which was sometimes same and sometimes different from their own opinion about themselves. Parents of Eighty percent students say that their child is not hard working or can be distracted very easily otherwise he/she is very intelligent. There have been cases when parents or the students themselves acknowledge that they are very bad at maths as a subject, though they were not, as I later taught them and found them to be very sharp. They later proved this also by their achievements and had made lasting impression on my mind. I found that every single child in the world is special. Everyone has something unique that defines oneself. Also everyone has strengths as well as weaknesses too. The need is of identifying strengths and to utilize them to better oneself in the task or even choose the task which demand these strengths and acknowledge the weaknesses so that you can overcome them. Here I'll tell you an experience. It was during 1998-99. My husband taught a student. The student was considered to be very weak in studies, tagged as below average students and moreover medically declared to be having limited mental abilities with no scope of any drastic improvement. His parents were very stressed, rather the correct statement would be, if I say, were forced to be stressed. They were totally hopeless. But he had many strong abilities, yet no one could notice him for those strong abilities. And he was intelligent too. His strong points were his sincerity, patience, respectful attitude towards elders and teachers, very social, and above all a very good listener. I always say that to be a good orator is quite easy but to be a good listener is very difficult. As an orator you are active and your instincts of being a speaker are also getting satisfied but while listening you are passive and are bound to listen to have some information or knowledge. So knowledge gaining is not that easy. He was always unperturbed even on getting scolded badly. My husband observed his qualities and conveyed it to his parents to not to worry, their child is unique in many aspects. My husband was sure that these qualities would take him long way. As a teacher he maneuvered his strengths to make him sail through dark waters. He did his post graduation, worked in MNC and today he stands as a mature, independent, settled man, holding greater ambitions. So focusing on strengths is a must. Your strengths can lead you to success. Some students are very laborious but not very sharp while some are very brainy, having quick grasping abilities but are not hard working. Only brain and no work cannot provide you much but an average student with lots of hard work can reach heights. If you have a sharp memory, you can cram things easily and fast, then you should be grateful that God has given you this special blessing. Every subject has a conceptual part, the theory, and then cramming and intelligence compliment each other in understanding any subject thoroughly with application. It can transform you from ordinary to extraordinary. Up to tenth class mathematics is a compulsory subject. I always say that Mathematics has its own language; if you try, you will definitely learn. To very weak students I suggest to cram questions with solutions. You become learned by doing so. Then you start to do more of them just by correlating. What you earlier have crammed (superficial then) is now imbibed. You start taking interest in the concerned subject, (here it is maths) and getting the subject. This change in the approach to take the subject is drastic one. Learn as you are to teach someone. It is the highest form of understanding. Teaching forces learning. When the teacher is teaching, actually two are learning and one is teaching. I have seen that mostly teachers don't allow students to see or check the answers given at the back of the book. Parents also tell them and strongly impose on them not to check the answers. This is a very wrong approach. They forget that self learning is actual learning. You go to school/tuitions for guidance. They guide you only. They can't implement on your behalf. They just tell you the right way and give the conceptual knowledge. So don't restrict kids from checking answers. By doing this, you are killing their curiosity to check that what they did was correct or not. Teach them to take it like a riddle or game. Imagine how curious we become to get know the correct answer of that. We also put our hundred percent (I can say, even more than hundred percent) to find answers. Deal with maths questions like these riddles. Check your answers from the book. If you find them to be correct, pat your back and move to the next. And if you find your answer to be wrong, try again and again until you get the correct answers or until you have tried all the possible ways. Look for similar examples and try again correlating and if your answer is still not matching, you can seek help from your teacher or anyone who can help you. One thing I take guarantee of is that you will start understanding and enjoying the subject. Your interest will be created in the subject. You will find that your fear of math, i.e., math phobia is gone. I am not saying that everyone will be transformed but I am not denying the possibility that everyone can be transformed.

We need to differentiate the hidden knowledge from ignorance, though they are demarcated by a very fine line. If we can train animals then how can we underestimate the capacity of human brain? Mind power should be given value. Our mind is always full of wonderful thoughts and novice ideas. We need to recognize that our thoughts have energy. The good thoughts keep us happy, strong and committed to goals while bad thoughts besides annihilating the power of mind, give the control over to others. So keep your mind healthy and strong. In the professional life, no one asks for your marks. Don't think that marks do not matter at all, but yes, it is true that only marks or grades lead you to nowhere. For career/ job the qualification is only the requisite for entry. It just gives you the opportunity to be considered. Everyone is running after success. Everyone wants to have it. But how can we find the path way to success? What we need to have our side? This all made me realise that I should pen down my conclusions which I made subconsciously, to inspire and motivate others out there to reach their goal, to share with everyone the qualities which I found very significant for success while teaching the very tender minds, to make change, to create transformation, to put a stop on blame game that I didn't get the chance to stop myself or maybe the stars and situation were not in my favour. Formal education is very necessary, yet it is not the measure of success. So all the variables (mentioned later) are like the input in the equation of success, by the term success here we mean it in a broader sense, not only at the academic level. To be successful we need to be educated; the education is judged not by the weight of degrees or certificates you are carrying, the education and schooling are two different things, we get education at home also. Everyone learns their first lesson at home and from parents/ family only.

Nothing succeeds like success. For a student to pass an exam with flying colours, is a success. And, for some other person, to establish his own business is a success. Still, for others to get a good white collar job is a success. Hence the definition and dimensions of success vary from time to time and person to person. The Person for whom at the age of eighteen, passing exams with good marks is a success and for the same person in his thirties, having established business or good job and well settled life is a success. With time as we grow older in age, parameters of success change and our outlook of success also change as well. Very few are born with silver spoon in their mouth which can be considered just like an admit card only in the exam of life, but not as the pass certificate. So hard work is very essential to get success and this hard work and perseverance is the struggle. Struggles beautify the journey. After one success we start running for the other. Hence struggle never ends. A blank page of life is always waiting to get written. Harder the struggle, more magnificent will be the success. Have you ever tasted success? Success is sweeter than sugar. But before every success is struggle. The sweat only brings sweetness. Here sweat is denoting the struggle and by sweetness, we mean the fruit, which is success.

Everyone says that nobody is perfect in this world. But it is also prevalent most of the times that one who is successful has no vice and the one who is a total failure has no virtue. A successful person needs not to tell others about his/her success, success itself makes noise. At the door of successful person are many relatives, but who shakes hand with the failure? Isn't it so that the success has many fathers but the failure is an orphan.

Everyone wants to be successful. Parents want to see their children successful in life. But there is no market from where success can be bought, it is rather earned. The definition of success is different for different people. If we go through the life histories of successful people we will see that success was not there on platter for them. Those people earned the success by facing all the challenges and never giving up. one thing I have realised that difficulties come in life to make you

'YOU'. And it is up to you. How do you view it? Do try the best at your end even for a very ordinary success. The sum total of all these small successes results in big achievement. If you stand up in every difficulty, then there is no such test that you cannot pass. Every man is architect of his own fortune. The success story has a body of attitude with the backbone of faith, scented with sweat. Anyone can write his own success story. There are three key factors, in addition to luck, to achieve the success. These three key factors are Faith, Attitude and efforts and one bonus factor, luck. Attitude and efforts are two wings and faith helps in flying by keeping the body streamlined. Here, by keeping the body streamlined we mean by providing direction, means navigation. It means that the key factors which I just mentioned are important as they actually form our strengths. But what about weaknesses? Nobody ever existed who had been absolutely flawless. Nature itself has been very fair in creating the balance everywhere and in everything. No single person you can say is having either all strengths or all weaknesses. Also this may happen many a times that the kind of behaviour, gesture etc. which we consider strength of one person is weakness of the other. If one person gets the benefit of keeping patience, may be some other person will be paying the cost of being patient. From this, it is concluded, though all the three key factors are equally important and are also inter-related, staying aware of our weaknesses is also very significant. You can't overlook them. How these factors are interrelated? You need to move in order. No chaosis, no zigzag. Follow the order. If you don't have first one, second one cannot be inculcated. It is also clear that to wear attitude you must have faith. Exactly without having second one, i.e., attitude, you cannot invest in the third one, viz to put in the efforts first you must wear the positive attitude which eventually will become a part of your personality. After the role played by the above three factors, We cannot deny the role of luck factor which actually provides you the opportunity. Without faith you cannot initiate, and without attitude and efforts, you cannot take the advantage of luck. Here the luck becomes the determining factor. Do not worry about the obstacles in the journey. Only make sure that the obstacles are not self-inflicted. Because the self-inflicted obstacles actually make your journey gloomy, sad and difficult. they squeeze you. And reveal anger, envy, distrust. But the unintentional, involuntary, forced or simply the obstacles which are not self-inflicted, actually keep you motivated, give you strength, beautify your journey, take out what is in us, make your life wonderful, and these are the ones which take you to the top. Otherwise, without these, I see them like this only, inspiring demons, either you would not be there at top or the top would have been overcrowded where anyone's presence hardly matters. Obstacles which are not self-inflicted put pressure which brings out the perfection and ultimately success. It is very important to learn the art of managing and apply the science of managing. Manage your strengths, weaknesses, time and life and by doing so you can make it a masterpiece.

Chapter II

Faith

The very first and very significant factor is faith which eventually leads to decision making. Let your conscience be your guide in making them. There is a great force hidden in faith. Only they conquer who think they can. And the thought process is influenced by the faith. It is very difficult or nearly impossible to initiate any task unless you have faith in that. If by chance it happens, then the Initiatives which are taken without faith are very soon dumped. Teachers always advise students to stay confident in the exams. This confidence is actually faith in its very simple form. It is faith in oneself. Faith is very well understood in the spiritual form. Swami Vivekananda ji, also, has quoted 'you cannot believe in God until you believe in yourself.' It reflects our faith in God. I will try to illustrate it with very common incidents where you can see how faith inculcates and transforms the future. Faith means faith in yourself, faith in God, faith in supreme power. It also means the faith in your deeds that whatever you are doing is right. Wrongs are never done with faith, they are always accompanied by fears. Faith is automatically formed when actually you are doing the right things in a right manner. Faith is foundation of morals. Young children should be educated about the faith from the very beginning. It will make them humble, grateful and able to withstand any difficulty or difficult situation with patience.

I was born in a vaishnav family. At a very young age, though I did not care very much consciously to learn how to have faith in myself, in God, but still I imbibed some ideas and thoughts, as my father used to tell the stories of God, demigods and other stories with moral values or having some message. I always saw and thought of him to be different from others not because he was my father, rather I realised, that he actually was different. The 'Be man' was a periodical published by Manavata Mandir, Hoshiarpur (Punjab) during those days. May be it is still in circulation but I am not sure. We used to get it at home by post and I used to read it as mostly all small stories, real incidents and quotes (mostly in urdu) were included in that magazine. In that book Faqir Chand Ji Maharaj, the first sant mat guru revealed that he had no knowledge of his form manifesting before a person and helping them with their worldly or spiritual problems. He openly emphasised that he has experienced that the real helper is one's own true self and faith. Here is an incident from the periodical 'Be Man'. Once a student in the examination hall did not know the answers to the questions. He got really scared that he's going to fail the exam. His parents were followers of manavata mandir. He had heard many stories of data dayal helping his devotees during the hard times. Children are very pure by heart and very good in imitating, they especially imitate their parents. If parents say anything to them, they do question it but also acknowledge whatever is told to them. So the boy had full faith in Data Dyal. Finding himself in this awkward situation, he was left with no option but to pray to Data Dyal Faqir Chand ji Maharaj whole heartedly with full devotion. His faith was strong. It was just like the faith of children in their parents. Eventually Maharaj ji appeared and made him write all the answers and the student passed in the examination. When he came to Data Dyal Faqir Chand Ji Maharaj to convey his gratitude towards him, he was shocked and speechless. Data Dyal Ji Maharaj said that he even did not know anything about his exam, rather he had been at his place (home) only. He emphasized that 'It was only your faith which helped you'. The boy was surprised to know all this. This was not that easy to believe and take it as some other story his parents and other followers tell him, but Maharaj Ji himself told him about it. These kind of true stories were generally told by my father and I myself experienced the same thing and concluded that if your faith is not shakeable, you definitely will reach the destination and achieve your goal. I am very much indebted to my father who gave me the first lesson on faith, even though he did it unintentionally. Faith can be a very powerful tool if you know when (during good times we have confidence due to faith but we should keep it as strong in tough times as well), where (in good deeds in a good way) and how (with a never complaining attitude, thinking positively) to keep it. Faith strengthens your relationship with God. Faith creeds are caught more than they are taught. Faith brings optimism and boosts the psychological wellbeing of a person.

In Punjab summers are very hot and winter are very cold. It was during 1983, the Schools were closed for summer vacations and we used to spend afternoons staying inside our homes because of the scorching hot weather outside. Mostly we used to play indoor games ludo or carom. One day while playing ludo, I was the first one to get a six on the dice. I will call the day special as later I got many sixes. By the time my first token was inside the home, my friends who were playing with me were trying to get at least one six so that they can start their game. Finally that day I won the game. I developed special connection with the yellow colour as my tokens that day were of yellow colours. I started noticing that whenever I choose yellow I win. Do you also feel so? No, I know it was just a matter of chance for you. But it worked for me during my ludo game. You might have heard people talking about their lucky charm, no? I started believing. And eventually my beliefs started taking the shape of faith during performances.

You can keep faith in an idea, in God, in your capacity or in a person. Before I write further, let me clear the difference between faith and trust. You can trust in a lot of things, but only in few amongst many, you can have faith. There is difference between faith and trust. Trust is a conscious trait and faith is unconscious one. Faith is a strong belief with trust, confidence and understanding. Faith is inexplicable. Faith is epitome of trust where you trust, not knowing the reason why you trust. Faith is looked upon as a spiritual concept. Trust means a firm belief in someone, complete confidence and reliance in another person. Faith is a noun. It is something you possess. Trust, on the other hand, is verb. It is an activity, something you do or act upon. Still faith and trust are interrelated.

There are many fables on power of faith. I came across this story by anonymous. Once there was a drought in a village. Villagers were told to ask God for rain as no other alternative was there since it is a natural phenomenon. All the villagers decided to gather to pray for the rain. A day of worship was selected on which they will do hawan, chant mantras, etc. On the day of prayer all the people gathered at the decided place. But one boy came with his umbrella as well. Everyone laughed and asked him why he brought the umbrella. The boy replied, "How will I go back when it will be raining heavily." This is faith. His belief was very strong that it will surely rain today. When parents play with their baby, they throw a baby in the air and the baby laughs because baby knows that parents will catch him. They will never let him fall. This is trust.

We should tell the children what is right and what is wrong. But do not develop their belief in wrong way. They should be able to distinguish right from wrong. I will explain with the help of an example; Junk food is not good for health but children are usually very fond of it, they actually relish it. It is not possible to keep them completely away from it but still limits can be drawn. They can enjoy it once in fifteen days or something like this. When your child is eating any kind of junk food, don't tell him/ her, 'since you are eating this, it is not healthy and you will get sick or it will harm you'. Don't induce the sickness in your kid. Don't tell your child that it is a bad thing rather tell that it is not good for health. Don't make the illness sure by developing faith out of fear. Mind's power influences our immune system. Mind is a very powerful tool that can make miracles happen. We need to learn how to use it properly.

Faith is the belief that is never questioned. Faith is the most powerful tool in making us who we are. To accomplish any task we need to put efforts but fifty percent task is done when we keep faith that it will definitely be done. Faith makes us go where we want to reach. The lack of faith makes us doubtful. A doubtful mind can't take decisions. If it does take decisions, one can't stay on those decisions for long. A doubtful mind keeps wavering and does not reach at any conclusion and finally gains nothing. Even the efforts one puts in to do something, goes wasted. Because all the energy, will etc. that was gathered to initiate the task, without faith, the patience to actually do the task got missing. And when the time came, and something good was about to happen, the wavering doubtful mind gave up as faith was lacking. The investment in other factors got wasted. Faith in God, faith in destiny, faith in being myself...faith plays a very significant role in all of our endeavours. I am a teacher and what I have seen is that students believe in their teachers strongly. They follow and learn even through the tough methods taught by their teachers, especially school teachers as compared to any other simple methods taught by any other person or given in any other book. It is all their faith in the teacher which develops a positive attitude for the various techniques, methods used by the teacher, which make them able to learn quickly. This behaviour is more prevalent in junior classes.

Faith gives hope, faith gives life, faith keeps you motivated, keeps you going. We when have no option, usually encourage people by saying 'have faith, everything will be fine'. These are really remarkable words. They have the capacity of turning someone's life around. Faith makes us hopeful and certain of what we cannot see. Faith cannot be purchased, sold, or gifted to anyone.

No doubt that the parents are the first teachers and the teachers are the second parents. Besides my first teacher, my mother was my maths teacher also (she was maths teacher), she has been my inspiration and role model. If I am asked to describe her in just two words; I will call her the 'Iron Lady'. Once my mother got severely ill, she was taken to the hospital and admitted there. Doctors were really disappointed to see her as she was weak and her condition was very bad. She was given around forty bottles of glucose and blood. By the grace of almighty, she recovered. When she was discharged from the hospital, the doctor himself said, "this lady defeated death." Doctors were hopeless in her case. Only medication was not the cause of her recovery. It was her faith, that she will recover, it helped her to overcome this situation. Due to certain circumstances I couldn't go to see her in the hospital. All I could do was the prayers while surrendering to almighty but only with faith. And I strongly believe that somewhere it was my faith that I can't afford to lose her right now at this moment of my life and so it will not happen. And she was back to her normal healthy life again.

Faith is substance of things hoped for when you need to make predictions or to know what is happening around you, its faith which helps you to come out as valiant. Faith helps us to make better predictions. Testing of our faith produces perseverance. It matures us. sometimes faith does not do what we want. It is just because our faith leads us to where we want to be and the faith that everything will go good and nothing really wrong will happen, this leads us to where we need to be. We all know the story of bhakt prahlad. It was only his faith in his God because of which he was not scared by any of the ordeal he had under gone. I am sharing this story of victory of faith by anonymous which I read on the internet. There was a very poor woman. She had a very small family. She called into a radio station and asked for help from God. she also mentioned her address. Call it by chance or the power of faith that a nonbeliever of God was listening to this on radio. He found it totally irrational. He thought of making fun of the dogmas.

He called his secretary and ordered her to buy food stuff etc. and take it over to woman along with some fair amount of money. But he instructed her strictly not to tell his name and if, by chance, she asks then tell her that it's from the devil. The secretary left for woman's house. The woman was very happy and grateful for the help that had been received. She did not ask anything about the sender. The secretary was confused. He himself asked her, "Don't you need to know about the person who sent all this?" The woman smiled and said, "Many thanks to whomsoever sent this! But I actually don't care who the person is because I am pretty sure when my Lord (GOD) orders, even the devil obeys!" The secretary was surprised to hear this. It is clear from this story, that with the beginning of faith, worries vanish. We can learn from the faith of others too. If life is filled up with faith and encouragement, it brings hope to others as well. No man is happy unless he believes he is. It simply tells us that faith, faith in good, faith in good deeds make the atmosphere vibrant, positive and brings optimism and peace.

If asked, most people will say 'Yes, we keep faith in God' but the question is how much faith? Once there was an old man, he fell ill and doctors diagnosed some serious disease. Doctors gave him medicine and to make him feel easy, they denied any serious illness and suggested him to pray to God and keep faith in Him as it is just age factor. The old man thought himself otherwise healthy. The old man was seeing things positively, making the prayers with full devotion and faith; he did not let any negative thoughts or doubts creep in his mind or heart. When he visited the doctor for follow up, the doctor was surprised to see him perfectly alright. It could only happen because there was no negative thinking or doubt; he thought positively and thinking is a biochemical process in which neurotransmitters chemicals are released; he trusted his doctor fully so could have firm faith in God. It affects our health. Learn to take care of your body. Don't focus on what you want not to happen. Most of the times people develop doubt in their faith and very fast situation changes from 'doubt in faith' to 'faith in doubt'. Now this faith in doubt becomes so strong that the whole aura of that person becomes negative with pessimism. Faith makes you strong and doubt brings fear with it. Faith does not reveal everything at once. Rather it gives enough strength, light to usher you to take the next step safely. The roots of faith need to be strong and deep enough to withstand the waves which bring doubt. Make your faith as firm as a rock. Don't keep any void for doubt to creep in. It's true that faith can move mountains but forget not that doubt can create mountains in your path. The hard times come uncalled. You need strength to restart. This strength comes from faith. Your faith keeps you focussed and helps you to stick to the initiative you have taken and finally leads you to success. When God pushes you to the most difficult situation trust him fully he will never let you down. Sometimes God sends you to places, where there is no light, only darkness; but do not think that you are being buried. You are dormant during that time and soon will awake and become active, get planted. Everything happens on time. Stop stressing yourself out. Keep faith that god is watching over you. And he will not leave you alone. Believe that his ways are perfect. Faith has power. You will continue to fail if you have doubt in every action you take, each decision you take. To do better, you have to develop faith first that you can do better. If you are always doubtful, start transforming your mind set. When the roots of faith are deep, there is no space for doubt left. Keep learning because life never stops teaching. Take on challenges. Life never stops; there is always a scope for new beginning or the ending can also be changed if only we intend for it to change, hence..... the show must go on.

Chapter III

Attitude

Blind turns of life should not stop you to move further. From here only a new inning can be started, a new history can be created. Don't take them as the one stopping you to move ahead, instead from here only you can start fresh, when you accept it as a new start, you find yourself full of energy. If you have not struggled, you cannot enjoy the success that much which you would have enjoyed otherwise. The wait, the hope for that wow kind of feel after crossing the tunnel to keep yourself alive. You can't feel the excitement in a smooth journey. It is attitude which keeps a person going and those who cannot support this kind of attitude they stop and only play the blame game. The blame is sometimes on family or friends, sometimes on circumstances and sometimes on destiny only. It only means that they have accepted the defeat which ultimately have stopped them to even try for the better one. It is the attitude only whether you feel old at thirty or young at eighty. Thinking you are sick can make you sick. It is all in the mind. The positive attitude has positive effect on our mind, so even biologically positive thinking result in outflow of positive chemicals from our brain and helps us getting better of the gloomy situation. The moment we develop a positive attitude, remotest of destination seems closer and achievable, and enhances our capacity to further our efforts. Small fears crippling our mind start vanishing. Power of mind is limitless, yet attitude is the key to unleash that power. Positive attitude is the killer of negativity. Positive attitude keeps you self motivated.

Engage your mind in the present and faith in the future. This will help you develop the 'Never give up' theory. Never give up, it does not matter how many times you have been knocked down, keep going. Perseverance is always rewarded. Your attitude defines you. Start being more positive. It is shown in the way you behave. It is your attitude which reflects how you manage yourself. Your attitude to different things is the way you feel and think about them. This attitude may be positive or negative. But generally when we say that a particular person has attitude, it means that he is confident or sometimes overconfident and tries to get noticed. It is your attitude which describes your vision. Eyesight is optional but the vision is mandatory for success. It is very difficult to change people's attitude. That's why we generally talk about attitude problem. We should be receptive in nature. We should have patience to listen and understand other people's way of thinking. On adding two to five we get seven but same we get on adding three to four too. It means there are a number of ways to do things. One needs to keep doors of mind open. And of course, should respect that. We can learn from others as well. In this way we can avoid many difficult situations. Every person thinks in his/ her own way. People have different tastes and interests. Different people have different mind sets. The same thing may be liked by one and disliked by other. Plant needs both sun and rain to grow. So both compliments as well as criticism should get acceptance. Both have impact on our growth. It will help you learn effectively and make you become successful. Life is not that simple. Learn to be happy right now otherwise you may run out of time. And to achieve this, positive attitude is a must.

It depends upon our attitude that how fast we can learn something. I have noticed this in the class that students with positive attitude put in hundred percent of their efforts to learn the topic while those with negative attitude only complain that they are not getting it. Actually they themselves have kept the doors of their minds shut. Your habits slowly get transform into your attitude. It is necessary that if you want to learn something, you must first accept that and then try. Then only it is easy. No one is born as a successful or an unsuccessful person. We are transformed according to how we think. The belief that all obstacles will be removed, inculcates winning attitude. It is the matter of attitude only that the same half filled glass of water is half filled for the one and half empty for the other.

The nature itself is the best teacher. We should learn from it and we of course do it unintentionally. You know patients in hospital if get a natural view from their hospital bed, they recover sooner than others. We all love nature. It helps in emotional regulation. It makes us positive thinkers. You can observe it simply. Strolling two kilometres on a road will make you tired and the same two kilometres stroll in the lush green park will freshen you up. You can also see the impact of nature on your attitude if you are travelling by train and you don't get the window seat. Everyone prefers the window seat. This shows that we try to remain close to nature as it keeps us happy and positive. Learn from the trees, birds, sky, ocean, moon and the sun etc. Trees stand deeply rooted in ground in all the conditions. Sky remains blue and let the transient storm pass by. Ocean tells us how the small parts make the greater whole. Tiny drops of water together make the ocean. Moon goes through different phases but always smile; and the sun keeps rising always, no matter how many times it goes down. We can learn from each and every constituent of nature. They give us most powerful lessons and make us learn that our attitude is up to us. Keep your eyes open to see the possibilities not the problems; and keep your mind open to visualize the things and not to find flaws in others or play cheap tricks. It is an old saying that a man is known by the company he keeps. But the man is also known by the company he avoids. Keep the company of your strengths and avoid the company of your weaknesses, you can transform them as well into your strengths. These all things add to your attitude which later form your personality. A man is the product of heredity and environment. Heredity, environment and the company these all are factors having contribution in your attitude building. In science we have learnt that part of universe which is under our observation is a system and the remaining is surrounding. Then we limit the surrounding by saying that for example if you are doing any experiment in the laboratory, then the apparatus you are using is the system and the laboratory is surrounding. No effect on system is significant by any factor beyond those four walls of laboratory. Same relation is between company and environment. We are most influenced by the surrounding people. Attitude is contagious. So develop healthy attitude and be the carrier. Attitude is that little thing which makes a big difference. A person once made a door especially for opportunity because he did not want the knock by any of them to be missed. This is the attitude. It is very often that any project started with positive attitude is always accomplished. Attitude is the thinking based on your experiences in life. Great personalities have great genes. It is believed that attitude is developed in DNA. Personality is inherent to some extent. Every person has set of traits blended together in which few are more dominating, from which personality of an individual can be predicted. Attitude influences our behaviour and can be changed only if you start accepting that it should be and it can be.

We can't speak about good or bad attitude. It will be just like blaming one another. Attitude can be positive or negative. Everyone has attitude of one form or the other. Also same person has different attitude to different problems. It is very rare that a person is having neutral attitude towards the issues of his/her interest or concern. Neutral attitude is seen only when the subject is neither of our concern nor of our interest. One's attitude is reflected in his/her behaviour. Positive attitude helps you to try to find the importance of things like smile, happiness, strength, courage, hope. It makes you optimistic and opportunistic too. If your attitude is positive, you will not spare any opportunity. I am a teacher. I have taught many students. But I got to learn many things from them. Till date I learn from my students. Let me tell you an experience. I wrote twenty questions of mathematics on a paper. At the top I marked it as an assignment and asked my students to solve all the questions. Most of the students were not ready to solve those questions because either they don't know or everything got messed up in their mind. Then I wrote similar twenty questions, only shuffled with numerical values changed, and marked on the question paper. I told them since that assignment was tough but here I give you a simple question paper, do solve it and I will evaluate it properly. They took assignment very lightly and left most of the questions unsolved even without trying. But in solving the question paper, they tried their level best, fighting for every single mark. Many students show the opposite behaviour. They are unable to solve those question which otherwise they could have solved, it is called examphobia. This shows the attitude how you perceive things. By only changing the attitude you can make big change in results. Attitude is the golden key which can unlock any door. Once a man was passing by the clothes show room. His eyes caught one of the dresses on the dummy. He liked it very much. He went inside the shop and asked for that dress. He tried but it was slightly tight. He asked for bigger size but shopkeeper told him that stock is over and it was the last one. But he can show him the other ones from the fresh stock. The man refused to select any other one from the fresh stock and bought that (small size, slightly tight) only. The shopkeeper was surprised and he could not resist asking the man. 'What will you do of this? Is not this smaller in size for you?' The man replied, "Yes, it is. But that's manageable. What If its size cannot be increased, I will work out in gym to bring myself to fit in this size and good shape." Now this is the attitude. It was just a dress but the man liked it so much and could not afford to lose it. He could make a way to work it out only because of his positive attitude.

Man is a social animal. Society, nature, surrounding atmosphere, all this has a great impact on his nature, on his behaviour. A child is born without any sense of fear, happiness, sorrow, anxiety and attitude. Attitude is not somethig some one is born with. It develops. I don't deny the role of genes but the surroundings' impact is much more. A child among men will soon be a man and a man among children will be long a child. You become what you feel. You start living that. You live well with positive attitude. It is better to live well than to live long. And actually who lives well lives long. Positive thinking keeps your aura strong. The one who lives with positive attitude will never be a loser, sooner or later s/he will be rewarded.

Once during a motivational speech, the orator invited the audience to play a game. He told them that they will be given slips, which they will fill in with information about their family, hobbies, income, assets and other things. Then the speaker will categorise them into rich and not rich categories. Those who wanted to play filled the slips. After collecting the slips from them, the speaker called the persons whom he considered rich on the stage. He evaluated richness in terms of different things like happiness, wealth, luxuries etc. One person whom he had not called on stage, stood up. He asked why he was not called on the stage though he is rich. The speaker asked his name, took out his slip and on seeing that he asked him to give at least the one reason why he should be considered rich? He called him on the stage. The speaker repeated the question. What made you think that you are rich? The person replied very confidently, "I have no debts and I am healthy." Hall reverberated with applause. This is the attitude. How you feel for yourself. How you take the things. How you measure the richness, happiness or success. Your attitude decides how you visualise the things. A lot of people are there who are happy in miserable conditions. Some do not have courage as they lack faith and try to justify failures. They have developed the attitude of giving up. your positive attitude can change your life forever. No person can handle every situation or knockdown every obstacle flawlessly, it is not that easy. But your attitude to visualise the things keeps your spirits high. Your attitude first helps you to face the problem and then solve the problem. Don't let the negative attitude suck your life. More you keep your attitude positive, more positive things will happen around you, with you. By now you should be more confident version of yourself. Mind is your greatest power. Keep it calm and stress free. Believe in it. Accept it. Wear the right and positive attitude. It creates happiness and success. Remember:

Positive Attitude → Positive Results

Chapter IV

Efforts And Hardwork

Any action is always better than no action. If you don't get the success, still you get the lesson. No one can teach better than an experience. Always remember what Lord Krishna had told Arjun 'Do your duty as Dharma and do not look for the rewards'. For starting any new venture, first you should have the faith that you are moving in the right direction, in a right way at the right time. Your strong faith will send you vibes that it is the best thing to do. The second factor is your positive attitude. It should be like this, yes, I can do this and definitely I will do this. Only they conquer who believe they can. Success is expected only when we take chance. Without pushing ourselves out of our comfort zone, we cannot have the exact information of our abilities. To take advantage of these, we need to put efforts and see where we have reached. Your dreams will not be served on platter. Don't forget that Today's tears water tomorrow's garden. Then only the continuous, rigorous efforts come into existence and take the shape of hard work. Don't waste your time while waiting for the ideal thing in an ideal way, remember that paths are automatically formed when you start walking and you leave the trail too. Follow the river, you will find the sea. There is no substitute for hard work. Only intelligence will not carry you so far. Without labour you can't achieve anything. Work first and then rest. You will never be betrayed by hard work. Don't be afraid of your mistakes, you will get the chance to learn from the mistakes you have done. Hard workers never complain. Even destiny surrenders to a person who never gives up and works hard and there is no gain without pain. Success does not come accidentally. Foot prints in the sand of time are not left by just sitting down, you have to walk over it. Very few people know how to do this. Only they conquer who make efforts. Efforts and hard work are like the spices which add flavour to the success; every rich or an established person cannot enjoy it when they are at this position just because of their rich parents or grandparents because any recipe without spices cannot be relished. Everyone should value it. Hard work always pays, you only need to identify your priorities. Once you note these, you can make a good strategy to work hard and achieve that goal. Success is sum total of efforts, perseverance, learning, sacrifice, steadiness. Efforts should be made not just for recognition but passionately for the accomplishment. While making efforts, put the sincere efforts believing only in hard work and forget the luck factor as luck only favours the doers. What luck or attitude brings, efforts will take away. Success is the sum of all the sincere efforts repeated again and again. Efforts is the saddle to ride out faith and attitude. If you have dreams, do efforts to make your dream possible. Success does not just happen. It happens because you put efforts to make it happen. Efforts which lead to big accomplishment are a series of small steps. An overnight success actually consumes many years. All you need is a goal, a dream in which you have complete faith and confidence which should be channelled onto the right path of action. When you start working for your dream to make it possible, it becomes goal. Having goal means you are committed and you will try to find the way and eventually reap bountiful from it. Otherwise, it will remain a dream only. Most people have dreams but not everyone has a goal. They only dream, they do not possess courage due to lack of right attitude, to try to change their dreams into reality. They end up blaming luck. So they have only dreams but they do not set the goals. Dream becomes goal only when you have faith in it and you start working for it passionately. You start pursuing them. The seed of success story is an idea and the fruit is success itself. This journey from seed to success is like a rollercoaster ride where safety is secured through faith, attitude and efforts. Your efforts may not be instantaneously rewarding but they never die. After the seed is planted, you have to wait for the fruit to eat. You stay patient and keep taking care of that seed grown into plant because you know and are sure enough that one day you will get the fruit. To know the value of hard work, first clear in your mind that hard work and work are actually two different things. When you work you get the result instantaneously. You cannot make an omelette without breaking the eggs. You were hungry, so you broke eggs cooked omelette and ate. But hard work means you are making efforts repeatedly to achieve something. You are the architect of your fortune. Efforts are your tools. Hard workers are not tale tellers. They really wonder to read their own success stories written by others. He who never tries never succeeds. Don't ever be scared of failure. He who never fails never succeeds.

What has been initiated with faith, carried along with attitude gets finally accomplished by efforts.

Keep this FAE (faith, attitude, efforts) strategy in all your endeavours. Stop trying to buy it. It can neither be bought nor be borrowed. You are to inculcate the attributes of this strategy, which you may find difficult in the beginning but eventually it will become a part of your nature and personality too. Faith is taking the first step when you even do not know the number of turns in the journey. This faith shapes the attitude rather it should be called positive attitude. It means you initiated it hopefully. Hope keeps your spirits high. It makes you capable of achieving anything you put your mind to. Whatever is done cannot be undone. Do not worry about the beginning, even if it is not good. You cannot change the beginning but you can make the end beautiful. Keep yourself focussed towards the goal with these three factors viz. faith, attitude, and efforts. it will definitely change the ending. Faith helps you to take decision to start any task and attitude will cause situations to come together in your favour. At last the chain of efforts lead to accomplishment. Keep moving forward with faith that all the efforts you are putting day in and day out, soon will provide you with fruit. Your time will definitely come. Do not be afraid of difficulties, once you pass over these situations, you no longer remain the same person who went in. Make your attitude very humble and positive. Besides it, a sense of gratitude must prevail. You will find yourself blessed. Replace your fears with faith and tears with sweat. Your faith will get you a chance, with attitude you can make it a choice and efforts will bring a change. Let no fear hold you back. Let no problematic thought defeat your efforts.

Chapter V
Luck

Always there is something higher and greater than individual which leads us in our endeavours. Faith, attitude and hard work are the three main factors of success. If we consider their contribution in success is 99.9% then remaining just 0.1% is contribution of luck, which can be the determining factor in bigger achievements. And yes, our luck is in our hands. We may call it opportunity. We can create our own luck by noticing the opportunities. The question is: luck favours whom? It does not favour one person over the other. The world is a trending place; if you can observe the trend then, yes, of course, you can allow more luck into your life. It depends how you address difficult situations. Luck favour those who are ready to take risks and work hard to achieve something. Don't ever compare yourself with others as there is no success in making comparisons. All learn differently and luck also matters. But hardworking optimistic people are not afraid of it. It is a matter of chance between equally hardworking people who have full faith in themselves and positive attitude towards the goal.

Luck smiles on such people. For others it is just an excuse, self-fulfilling prophecy.

I don't believe in luck very much. Luck without hard work (faith and attitude are there then only hard work is considered) is short lived. It provides you a chance only. But I do believe in the supreme power. For me the luck is the measure of His extra grace, we can take it like a bonus. But not to forget that 'God always help those who help themselves,' from this I only conclude that luck favours the doers, the hard workers with positive attitude. We create our luck by our thoughts and behaviour.

I have heard a story of a girl (an athlete) who got sick before the championship. What about practice? She was not even able to walk without support. She pleaded the doctors to make her well soon so that she can participate in the championship. The doctors assured her that she would be able to participate definitely as by the time of the championship she will get fit. 'But without practice! how will I be able to crack it?' she was not ready to accept the defeat after participation. She took the decision. While she was bed ridden in the hospital, mentally she started preparing from there only. She rehearsed in her mind only. It was her routine for the whole month before the event. Her mental learning was transferred to physical performance. When the day came, she participated in the race. She was confident, hopeful and cheerful. To everyone's surprise she won the race. When asked, she called it 'mind power' as she started rehearsing in mind. She did it regularly and stayed focussed to win the race. One thing is clear that action excels inaction. If she had not participated, she would not have won. Her attitude was very positive. When she was not able to do anything, she started practicing in her mind. And it was her faith that kept her motivated. A genuine good amount of faith, attitude and efforts got blended properly with luck and ultimately resulted in her success. The girl won by luck but if she would not have tried, luck would not have favoured her. To achieve massive success, you need to believe in your success before achieving it.

The key factors which I explained above are faith, attitude and effort. First, I take the 'faith'. When it is faith in God, it strengthens us. If it is in oneself then it may be our strength or weakness. To make it strength we should be very well aware of complexity of faith as when we keep faith in ourselves it becomes confidence. From confidence it can easily become under confidence (insufficient confidence) or over confidence (excess of confidence) which will add to our weaknesses. If over confident, person consider himself/herself better than others and under confident are not comparable. They are 'I cannot', 'I will not' type of people. Confidence is a good trait. If you are true to yourself, your faith in yourself will be confidence and will remain a strength only. The second one is attitude. It means you should be a positive thinker, which does not mean that you move away from reality. By being a positive thinker means you will find a way out whatever the situation may be.

Positive thinking is our strength and the negative thinking is our weakness. So quit negative thinking. Negative thinking stops us from doing anything. It creates fear in us. Therefore think positively, face the situation and look for the alternatives. Your positive approach will help you explore and you will find something worthy and perhaps exciting too. Next is hard work, how much efforts you put in? thinking and analysis is okay but don't waste your time and energy on overthinking and over analysing the things. Most people do this as they are having fear inside of making mistakes. The best way to deal with it is by making your mistakes your teacher. They will teach you the best lesson. Now we come to action. You should set the goal for each day. "Take care of the pence and the pound will take care of themselves'. One more is; 'Take care of minutes and the hours will take care of themselves.' Follow the same thing. Focus on your daily goal. You will not have to be worried about the final big goal- the success. Don't put off the things till tomorrow because it never comes. And it is the first sign of shirkers. Pull it off and start working honestly for the goal. You are now at the door step of success only waiting for the opportunity. Inside somewhere you know that you will not let that go. You have worked for that keeping all this in mind and finally you will get what you have been longing for, working for. And when someone asks you about your success and the story behind it, you tell that I just tried my hands on this and luckily I achieved. You are happy, more than happy, you want to celebrate your achievement. You know why you feel so? Because everything was well organised. You managed it properly so you did not feel the burden, no pressure, for you it was just routine and you thought that you found it easily. But reality is that it was not easy but you worked smartly with sincerity and passion. Be honest to yourself. What does it mean? It will be clear from what I am going to write now. The easiest way to stick to your goal is to make the announcement. Now other people know this as you yourself have declared. If you value your words, you will find yourself accountable to accomplishment. Hence you become determined. Now you are not only dreaming, you have a goal. Faith, in the goal, will keep you motivated. It helps you to develop the positive attitude which ultimately creates happiness in the atmosphere and to-do attitude in the healthy environment, keep you engaged in making the efforts. What can be uncomfortable in the beginning, later you will enjoy that because you are sure of your success. Your faith makes you determined and the efforts you put in give satisfaction. Try to create change in your life. While we are about a step away from our destination and look back; we have a reason to smile and find out that our faith kept us going, our attitude kept us alive, and efforts lead us to sail through. The three ingredients mixture of faith, attitude and effort creates quantum force that drives us along any terrain unshakeably. And it attracts good luck.

Every problem has a solution. Seed of solution is in the problem itself. No lock has been made without key. You can beat all the odds. Nothing is stronger than you. You only need to focus on your goal and at the same time you must acknowledge your weaknesses. Without doing so, you cannot work on them and transform those into your strengths. Stop running from your weaknesses. Weaknesses create a kind of fear in you. And you cannot learn anything out of fear while learning is key to success as it provides us with knowledge. This is the struggle which never means failure. Struggle is not your enemy, it is your teacher. It carries the hidden blessings. To find them you need to unfold it. It will strengthen you and later will define you. Don't give up on it and let it destroy you. Be the maker of your destiny. Successful persons have certain qualities. Apart from hardworking, they are goal oriented, dedicated and well prepared. Try to imbibe these qualities into your personality. You will find that you have been transformed into a better version. In the last, I want to summarise it as:

Believe...Wear the attitude and put in the efforts...achieve...succeed...you are in the category of lucky people!

About the Author :

Post graduate in chemistry (Guru Nanak Dev University, Amritsar) with B.Ed, teaching maths past thirty years, very fond of reading, especially life histories of great people, 'shayari' is something that takes her beyond horizon, has been through many 'a good' and 'not so good' times in life but always cheerful and a person with a 'never give up' attitude, also a poetess and a lyricist (song 'yaadein' released by overshadow creations),her book ' KITABE E ZINDAGI' is out in the market .

You can contact her through mail id ashus1223@gmail.com